Black Beans, Mean Business
third edition

a survival guide for struggling entrepreneurs

by
Michael Lombardi

Black Beans

Dedication

To those who dared to bear with me through the insanity.
It may not have paid off just yet, but at least now you'll have an
idea of what I *really* went through.

Black Beans

Contents

Black Beans

Forward

The black bean...

Merely a common food product in the pantry to most, and while generally not referred to by its more honorable categorical identity – the legume; this is no ordinary food.

The black bean is legendary by allegiance. They are pure protein, providing the raw power to move mountains with gumption and tenacity. The entrepreneur finds identity, comfort, compatibility, and refuge within the black bean. Small but significant, and capable of providing a life sustaining force, these two - entrepreneur and black bean - are one.

It feeds the hungry human vessel; nourishing the body and mind of the ravenous few who dare to dream. This synergy, of bean and man, is nutrient enriched by design and empowered to deliver markedly definable and measureable results.

The author, Michael Lombardi, is "the black bean" and many others like him embody these very same ideals. This work, 'Black Beans, Mean Business', is a tribute to the strength and tremendous value found within this nutrient enriched food, as it sparks and enables the entrepreneurial spirit to speak and thrive from within.

 Enjoy!

-Don Goulart Jr.
(March 2010)

Black Beans

Introduction

I've always been a free-thinker, a dreamer, and creative type person. It all started back in kindergarten, where I was so infatuated with Native American culture, that I dressed the part (despite my Italian and Polish heritage), at school, wearing my headband, moccasins, and poncho...no, it was not Halloween, this was my typical Monday through Friday. The creative spell carried over to first grade, where I was deeply entrenched in playing with Lego's. These magical building blocks freed my mind, allowing innovation at a ripe young age. In fact, this sparked my first lesson in intellectual property rights. At one point, I 'invented' a Lego person dressed as a SCUBA diver, and with the help of mom, sent the prototype and a letter to the Lego people. I received the classic feedback..."thank you for your wonderful ideas, unfortunately we cannot accommodate every request". Some 15 years later, sure enough, SCUBA Lego's hit the streets. If only I knew then, what I know now...that would've been my 'widget', and my life would've been changed forever. Maybe the Lego people are listening...

Black Beans

At age 10, I was taken by UFO conspiracy, and founded my first club organization, the 'Special Investigations Committee on UFO Sightings' or 'SICUS'. The fad lasted only 4-6 months, and was met with skepticism by classmates and teachers. However, my library research at the time, combined with a number of observations, led to mailing a compilation of 'sighting reports' to a certain government agency. It was received, obviously looked at, and returned. Had I cracked the code?

Without boring you with my many creative and entrepreneurial exploits, all beginning at a very young age, my point is this - those who are entrepreneurial in spirit, have been for their entire lives. It has only been sheltered by the 'normalcy' of the daily grind. Think back, it's true. This creative spirit and drive is inherent in human nature, yet there are few, who despite mass societal conformity, stray from the masses, follow their dreams, and realize success at all cost. It's more than thinking outside the box, it's about creating your own box, or process, which drives the evolution of your vision as it materializes. In harnessing your individual potential, shoot for the moon and you will influence a small piece of the world that you can call your own, and maybe even leave some small legacy in the process. That is where you will find your truest self, strength in that, and only then will you be satisfied. You have no choice but to do this.

This text is dedicated to you... You are the now recently dumped or divorced, nearly bankrupt visionary, who has over leveraged all of your credit cards, are negotiating with your landlord on doing yard work in lieu of paying rent this month, borrowing stale bread from your neighbor to put a PBJ in your belly, checking e-mail while sitting outside of the local coffee shop since your wireless service got cut off and you can't afford to go in and actually buy a coffee, and depending on those leftovers from family gatherings to survive through the next 3-4 days. You wake up every morning not knowing how to cut it through the end of the week, living in fear of the repo man, yet refuse to 'get a real job'.

Why?

Because you know you've got what it takes - all this is temporary. You're widget is the best thing since cell phones, and by cutting through the masses and sticking it out, you are climbing the ranks of the elite, becoming noticed amongst your peers...you are creating YOUR legacy. You know that it isn't what you take with you, rather it's what you leave behind. You isolate yourself from 'the real world' because it brings you down; it makes you, the visionary, the type of person that created their world, feel like you are wasting your time - yet you persist.

You have no choice.

You wake up day after day begging for start-up money, writing 17 drafts of a business plan, that you can't afford to make copies of for your upcoming investor meeting, so you sell all of your assets, before they become targets for your creditors, buy some paper, a few days worth of groceries, and pay one bill that's sitting on top of the file folder with more than 100 overdue bills...and then your ink cartridge goes south at page 4 of the first copy.

Black Beans

You are operating in the dark, the shadows of society, but building, creating, and making a difference. All you've got is the shirt on your back and a few friends willing to buy you a beer on the weekend. But you're here because you want to be, because there is no other option. You've dodged the bullet every day, and you've lost the consoling significant other, but who needs'm anyway.

As if your 18 hour days, every day, for the last 4 years weren't enough with all the doors slamming in your face...you've stretched beyond the critical point of survival, and mental clarity is at risk of being lost.

Yet you are still breathing, somehow you have a roof over your head.... You have you, and your idea, a copy of this book, and now you will be able to eat.

Here, I offer you 'Black Beans, Mean Business'. Amidst my quest of pursuing my vision, and meeting several missions in the process, I discovered the near perfect food - black beans. I survived, quite literally, on black beans for the majority of almost 2 full years, with little exception. They are the perfect legume, with capabilities ranging from soup to desert. Here, I share my secrets for survival, and many favorite recipes to this day.

Coupled with one unique recipe for each day of the week are a number of basic business tips, along with some motivational and inspirational quotes from those who sculpted the world we live in... after all, you're next, right? You may as well take advice from those who have been in your shoes. So - chin-up, take a breather, grab a can of black beans, and ENJOY!

Chapter 1
About Black Beans

Black beans, scientific name *Phaseolus vulgaris*, are also commonly referred to as frijoles negros, turtle beans, Spanish beans, Tampico beans, and Venezuelan beans.

Their basic characteristics include being about the size of a pea, up to ½-inch long, and are oval in shape, and up to 1/2-inch long. Black beans are a variety of the kidney bean, but with a slightly less-pronounced boat-shape. They are nearly jet black with a cream colored flesh, a mild, sweet, earthy taste, and a soft texture. When cooked, the flavor is strong and slightly sweet, with a mildly creamy texture.

Black beans have long been a protein-rich staple food of many Latin cultures. Today, black beans are enjoyed by most cultures around the world, and are a mainstay in most kitchens.

Black Beans

History

Black beans are native to the Americas, and are thought to have originated in southern Mexico and Central America over 7,000 years ago. Evidence of black beans has been found in excavations of prehistoric dwellings. The black bean has since spread widely around the world, and is most regularly used throughout Latin America, the Caribbean, and the southern United States. Black bean soups, stews and sauces are very common in Latin American countries. Black beans are becoming more popular in this country (US), in part due to increased immigration from Latin American countries, and their respective culinary traditions.

Although Latin Americans have long used black beans in soups, stews, and chilis, the Coach House restaurant in New York City is credited with expanding the popularity of black beans in America with their famous black bean soup that was first cooked up in the 1970's.

Black beans are now also popular in bean salads, bean soup mixes, bean pancakes, and as refried beans. The Brazilian national dish, *feijoada*, celebrates black beans in a hearty meat stew which is consumed by most Brazilians nearly every weekend. The Cuban dish *Moros y Cristianos*, or Moors and Christians, is a dish of black beans and white rice traditionally served on New Year's Day for good luck.

Growing Characteristics

Black beans grow best at temperatures between 65 and 75 degrees Fahrenheit. They are a warm season crop, requiring up to four months to reach maturity. The beans are typically left on the plants to dry. However, humidity and heat can cause damage to the beans as they are drying on the plant, and rain can be a problem during the drying and curing process. They are harvested by machine, and the plants themselves are left to re-fertilize the soil.

Selection and Storage

Black beans come in dried form and are not eaten fresh. The beans must be soaked, reconstituted, and cooked before eating. When buying bulk dried black beans, buy only as much as you will use in a month. When purchasing dry beans in bulk, avoid chipped, or cracked beans, and those with excessively chipped skins. Tiny pinholes in dried beans indicate a bug infestation, and should thus be avoided.

Dry black beans keep well for over a year in an airtight container. When re-stocking, do not mix new beans with any remaining older dried beans. They will cook at different rates, with older beans taking longer to cook.

Canned cooked black beans can be a real timesaver. They can be used interchangeably with dried beans in most recipes. Canned beans should be drained and rinsed before using. Unopened canned beans should be used within 1 year.

Cooked beans should be refrigerated and used within a week. To freeze cooked beans, first drain them and then place in an airtight container. Use frozen cooked black beans within 6 months.

General Preparation Methods

Whether you are using dry-packaged or canned beans, the following tips from the Bean Education & Awareness Network (B.E.A.N.) will ensure the best tasting beans for all of your favorite recipes.

Cleaning Dry-Packaged Beans
Before cooking, be sure to pick through them, picking out any small pebbles, split or cracked beans, and any other foreign matter. (Beans from the Rockies and Pacific coast tend to have bits of clay and stones). It is also helpful to cover the beans with cold water, let them sit for 5 minutes and then remove anything that floats. Repeat the rinsing process to be sure all dirt and foreign matter is removed. Drain this water before continuing with the soaking process.

Soaking Dry-Packaged Beans
After the cleaning soak/rinse, dry-packaged beans can be soaked to help soften and return moisture to the beans. This will reduce cooking time. Most beans will rehydrate to triple their dry size, so be sure to start with a large enough pot.

- *Hot Soak and Quick Soak*
  Hot soaking helps dissolve some of the gas-causing substances, making the beans easier to digest. For each pound of beans, add 10 cups hot water, heat to boiling, and let boil 2 to 3 minutes. Remove from heat, cover and set aside for at least one hour (Quick Soak), or up to 4 hours (Hot Soak).

- *Traditional Overnight Soak*
  For each pound (about 2 cups) of dry-packaged beans, add 10 cups cold water and let soak overnight, or at least 8 hours.

Cooking Dry-Packaged Beans

Drain the above soaking water and rinse the beans one last time. Beans should be cooked in fresh water. In general, beans take 30 minutes to 2 hours to cook depending on variety. Check bean packaging for specific cooking times and instructions.

Spice up beans while they cook. Seasonings such as garlic, onion, oregano, parsley or thyme can be added to the pot while the black beans are cooking. Add acidic ingredients, such as tomatoes, vinegar, wine, or citrus juices, should only be added at the end of cooking, when the beans are tender.

Add salt only after beans are cooked to tender. If added before, salt may cause bean skins to become impermeable, halting the tenderizing process. Further, black beans have a naturally strong and delicious flavor that is often accented with acidic ingredients which are common to Latin American and Southwest US style cooking. Salt is generally not needed.

To test for complete cooking, bite-taste a few beans. They should be tender, but not overcooked. When cooling, keep beans in their cooking liquid/sauce to prevent them from drying out.

Black Beans

Cooking With Canned Beans
Canned beans are a great convenience since they are already presoaked and precooked. Always drain and thoroughly rinse canned beans before adding them to a recipe. It is not necessary to re-cook canned beans, just heat them if a recipe calls for it. Canned beans, like dry-packaged beans, absorb flavors from other ingredients in a dish because their skins are completely permeable.

Chapter 2
Recipes for Success

This collection of recipes is something special to me personally. They are all incredibly simple, and particularly delicious. I've found that simple variations in seasoning, or when served in varied arrangements and accompaniments, make the simple black bean highly versatile. All recipes in this book are described using canned, pre-cooked beans. For the busy entrepreneur, this is the only reasonable way. Fresh, dry beans take a significant time commitment to prepare for cooking. When time is of the essence, rely on innovation just like in other aspects of life. In this case – the can.

Coupled with one recipe for each day of the week are a number of business tips that I've collated over the years, all boiled down to their simplest form. These are all applicable in for-profit and non-profit businesses, individual projects, or micro-ventures. When things are getting seemingly complicated, sit back, grab some black beans, and revisit the fundamentals. The clarity provided might be just what you need at a critical point in time.

"If you can dream it, you can do it."
-Walt Disney

Food for Thought
Do what you can with what you've got. Train yourself how to make money. Got ten bucks, make it twenty rather than spend it.

Remember, you are a producer, not a consumer. The consumer is your client, and you have a product/service that they need.

Monday | Mikey's Classic Black Beans

Ingredients
- 1 15oz can black beans, drained and rinsed
- ¾ cup minced yellow onion
- 1 HEAPING tablespoon minced garlic in water
- 2 tablespoons corn oil
- 1 tablespoon chili powder
- 1 tablespoon oregano
- ¾ cup apple cider vinegar
- fresh ground pepper to taste

Preparation Instructions
Heat corn oil in a medium saucepan. Brown the onions and garlic. Add the black beans, mix, cover the saucepan and reduce heat to medium. Let the beans cook for five minutes or so. Keep an eye on them. If the pan is too hot, they will stick. Add the chili powder, oregano, and cider vinegar, then cover and let simmer until you see little bubbles poking through the beans, probably another 15-20 minutes. At this point, they are ready to eat. I prefer to keep the heat low, and slow cook them for a half hour to forty five minutes until they thicken up.

Serving suggestions
This is my black bean staple. They can be served by themselves, or with a pile of cheddar or jack cheese, or a dollop of sour cream. The beans can be served with rice, with chips or nachos, on a baked potato, you name it. My favorite way to serve these is folded inside a corn tortilla with some cheddar cheese. I then drench them with my favorite hot sauce.

"Out of clutter, find simplicity. "
-Albert Einstein

Food for Thought
Establish both active and passive modes of income. Small, but regular passive incomes help offset your routine expenses, and in time provide enough money to invest into your projects. For example, royalties on IP are long-term sources of passive income. Interest from an endowment or a high interest account is also passive. Active income includes payments for goods and services.

Tuesday | Mexi-Black Beans with Cilantro

Ingredients
- 1 15oz can black beans, drained and rinsed
- ¾ cup minced yellow onion
- 1 HEAPING tablespoon minced garlic in water
- ½ of a fresh jalapeño, minced
- 1 handful of fresh cilantro, finely chopped
- 2 tablespoons corn oil
- ½ tablespoon chili powder
- 1 teaspoon cumin
- ½ cup apple cider vinegar
- fresh ground pepper to taste

Preparation Instructions
Heat corn oil in a large skillet. Brown the onions, garlic, and jalapeño. Add the black beans, mix, and reduce heat to medium. Let the beans cook until they appear to start breaking down. Add the dry spices, and the cilantro, mix. Then add the cider vinegar. Keep everything moving so it doesn't stick to the pan, and cook them to be on the dry side, like refried beans.

Serving suggestions
I typically serve these as a side dish with Mexi- food, however they are also delicious by themselves with chips or a pile of nachos. Leftovers can be used to make 'dirty eggs' for breakfast. Re-heat the black beans in a skillet until they are really sizzling, then add a few eggs. Scramble the eggs in with the beans. Serve in a breakfast burrito, or by themselves with some salsa.

"Determine that the thing can and shall be
done, and then we shall find the way."
-Abraham Lincoln

Food for Thought

Attack your business as a 'project' that has a well defined
beginning, middle, and end. With this outlook, it will be easier to
let go of if/when that time comes. You are a visionary, and you
are on a mission! It's all about getting the mission
accomplished. In many cases, this will require financial
assistance, infrastructure, and other support from already
established entities or individuals, in which case, you might
have to let go of some control. This is perfectly ok, just be
prepared for the self-inflicted struggle to be faced with in
watching your baby grow up.

Wednesday | Black Bean Soup

Ingredients
- 1 15oz can black beans, drained and rinsed
- ½ of a sweet onion, chopped
- 1 HEAPING tablespoons minced garlic in water
- 2 stalks of celery, chopped
- 3 carrots, peeled & chopped
- ½ cup chopped sundried tomatoes
- 1 Serrano pepper, minced
- 1 15oz can of chicken or vegetable stock
- 1 cup of balsamic vinegar
- 1 teaspoon chili powder
- 3-4 strips of bacon (optional, but *really* good)

Preparation Instructions
In a skillet, cook bacon. Remove and drain the fat, then chop the bacon. To the now seasoned skillet, add the onion, garlic, peppers, and sundried tomatoes. If not using bacon, use corn oil to sauté these veggies. Cook until tender, then add the balsamic vinegar and cook for another minute or two. Add this mixture, and all remaining ingredients, including the chopped bacon, to a crock pot or large saucepan. Add water until all of the ingredients are covered, and the soup seems to be at a reasonable volume. Cook on low heat until the carrots are tender.

Serving suggestions
Serve garnished with a sharp cheddar or jack cheese, or with a dollop of sour cream. Crumble tortilla chips on top for some texture.

"Do, or do not. There is no 'try'."
-Yoda

Food for Thought
LEVERAGE, LEVERAGE, LEVERAGE. Small victories will lead you to be triumphant over the major battle. Leverage your small successes when pursuing the next step, and don't be afraid to make a small step your short-term priority. Your sense of achievement in small stages will boost morale. These small successes all lend to increased credibility in your community.

Thursday | BB's on Toast

Ingredients
- 1 15oz can black beans, drained and rinsed
- ¾ cup minced red onion
- 1 green pepper, chopped
- ½ cup chopped sun-dried tomatoes
- ¾ cup balsamic vinegar
- ¾ cup tomato sauce
- 1 teaspoon chili powder
- 1 tablespoon oregano
- 2 tablespoons corn oil
- fresh ground pepper to taste
- a few slices of your favorite bread, toasted

Preparation Instructions
In a large skillet, add corn oil, and cook the onions, peppers, and sun-dried tomatoes on high heat until tender. Add the black beans and cook for another minute or two. Add dry spices and balsamic vinegar. Continue to cook on high heat until the beans appear to start breaking down. Add tomato sauce and reduce heat to a simmer.

Serving suggestions
In New Zealand, baked beans are often served on toast. This is a staple prepared in nearly every household. By cooking black beans with a sweeter, tomato based sauce, we gain the texture of the baked bean, but preserve the rich and bold flavors of the black bean. Serve a healthy ladle full over toast. This is comfort food at its finest.

"I find that the harder I work,
the more luck I seem to have."
-Thomas Jefferson

Food for Thought
Let the numbers tell the story. Don't even bother with the text for a business plan, until you work your numbers. They are EVERYTHING. Boil is right down to the basics: income & expenses. Revisit the core parts of your business in the numbers. You'll be surprised at how easily 'extra' expenses add up. Keep it simple, and stay true to the story that the numbers tell.

Friday | Black Beans & Rice

Ingredients
•About a half a batch of leftovers from Monday's Mikey's Classic Black Beans.

•one large beefsteak tomato
•Kosher salt
•one cup of brown rice

Preparation Instructions
Add the leftover black beans to a large skillet, and reheat until bubbling through the beans. If they are dry, add a cup of water and a half cup of cider vinegar. Stir in one cup of brown rice, and ensure that the rice is completely covered with liquid. Cover, and cook at medium-low heat. As the rice absorbs the fluid, stir in more water to bring up the volume, again covering the rice and beans. Continue this process until the rice is tender and done. The cooked rice and beans will be on the sticky side, and piping hot.

Serving suggestions
Serve a pile of these black beans and rice on a plate and top with your favorite hot sauce. Add several thick slices of lightly (kosher) salted beefsteak tomato alongside the rice and beans.

"I have learned, that if one advances confidently in the direction of his dreams, and endeavors to live the life he has imagined, he will meet with a success unexpected in common hours."
-Henry David Thoreau

Food for Thought
Forge relationships and partnerships horizontally within your industry. Today's small business climate has evolved to embrace collaboration. Collaboration affords access to resources that might take years to acquire on your own. Your cooperative efforts can be leveraged for vertical successes, which are a win-win for you, your colleagues, and your community.

Saturday | Black Bean Dip

Ingredients
- 1 15oz can black beans, drained and rinsed
- ½ cup of your favorite salsa
- ½ cup fat free plain yogurt
- small handful of finely chopped fresh cilantro
- 1 tablespoon of finely chopped jalapeño (optional)
- ½ teaspoon cumin
- hand squeezed juice of 1 lime

Preparation Instructions
Add the black beans and salsa to a blender or food processor and pulse to coarsely cut the ingredients. Add to a bowl, along with the remaining ingredients. Store chilled, but let stand for half an hour before serving to come up to room temperature.

Serving suggestions
This black bean dip is best Served with tortilla chips, or with a pile of nachos. This dip can also be used as a topping for a quesadilla, or even as a sandwich spread.

"Success is not measured by what a man accomplishes, but by the opposition he has encountered and the courage with which he has maintained the struggle against overwhelming odds."
-Charles Lindbergh

Food for Thought
Think grassroots baby. You are starting on the ground, and in the trenches. Every person you personally come into contact with is an opportunity to share your brand – your identity. Don't be pushy, but hold your head high, and be confident. You are here because you want to be. Find peace with this place that you find yourself, and draw from your environment, rather than be distracted from it. Channel this positive energy. It will go noticed amongst your friends, family, and peers.

Sunday | Black Bean & Corn Salsa

Ingredients
- 1 15oz can black beans, drained and rinsed
- 1 cup minced sweet Bermuda, or Vidalia onion
- 1 15oz can (use bb can) of frozen yellow corn kernels
- 2 HEAPING tablespoons minced garlic in water
- 2 medium sized vine ripened tomatoes, chopped
- a handful of fresh cilantro, chopped
- hand squeezed juice of 2 limes
- 1 teaspoon kosher salt
- 2 tablespoons corn oil
- ½ of a fresh jalapeño, minced, or more per your liking

Preparation Instructions
Mix onion, garlic, tomato, black beans, and corn thoroughly in a large bowl. Add cilantro, lime juice, salt, and corn oil. Mix gently. Refrigerate in covered container for 3-4 hours before canning/serving.

During summer months, use all farm fresh or organic ingredients for an incredibly fresh and crisp taste and texture.

Serving suggestions
Well, you've made it through the week, so this recipe is a real treat. My recommendation is to make a double batch. I've found that once people dig in, it's hard to keep their hands out of the bowl. I've eaten a bowl of this as a meal in itself, almost like a gazpacho. Serve with chips, as a garnish for a quesadilla, or even as a side to compliment grilled chicken or fish. I guarantee you will not be disappointed with this one.

Black Beans

Chapter 3
Down to Business

Naturally, there are far more comprehensive resources and texts on business start-up and entrepreneurship than this one. My objective in writing this section, and this entire text, was to provide some insight and a sense of uplift as you trek along at the very early stages of your venture. For this final chapter, I decided to focus on what I feel to be the single most important element in getting your idea out there...the elevator pitch.

You can have the greatest idea in history, but unless it gets in front of the right people, be it an investor, a manufacturer, a key distributor, a bank, or customer, it will sit right there on your desk where the idea was born and have no chance of making it into the real world. Now, there are of course critical steps to take well before spurting what could be a premature idea out there. It could be fatal to not take the time to well develop the idea, the financial prospects, actually define the product or service, and thoroughly understand the industry you are trekking out into. But, when the time is indeed right, you need to have your story buttoned up tight.

This doesn't always happen on your first, second, or even third pitch to an investor, donor, sponsor, or first customer. So, be humbled and mindful of your infant beginnings, and practice, practice, practice.

Presentation is everything.

Most entrepreneurs have heard about the "Elevator Pitch", which is classically defined as how to describe your great business opportunity in 30 seconds or less. This pitch is not going to close a deal, rather it opens a door. Once that door is open, you can start building a relationship that may, or may not, end in the results you expected or were originally hoping for. That's perfectly ok. You made a critical contact, and this will ease the pain in opening the next door. Remember those small successes, they make a huge difference.

Before I outline what information you should present to a potential investor, or donor, it's important to understand your situation. First off, the initial meeting is just that - an initial meeting. If you keep your audience captive for those 30 seconds, it shows that the investor has some interest in your idea, but that's about it. You have to build a trusting relationship before actually popping the question, and especially before closing a deal. Second, most investors and donors have busy schedules. Be concise, but not pushy, and let them ask questions. Let your audience guide you so you understand what exactly they are looking for. Generally, they want to make money (an investor) or a measureable improvement of the quality of life for a community or industry of interest (donor).

If you've got what they want, your first meeting could be an exceptional one and they will make time to continue to work with you.

Bottom line is to be patient, concise, and well-educated on what you are proposing. Finally, be sure to have at least a little bit of knowledge in each of the following nine key topics that I've identified as critical components to the elevator pitch. Keep this knowledge in your back pocket at all times so you aren't caught off guard.

The Nine Key Topics to Keep in Your Back Pocket

When you have a captive audience, be it for 30 seconds, or an hour, it is so important to touch on *all* aspects of the business or project. This means more than just a detailed look at the widget or some grandiose idea to save all of humanity's problems. Your audience needs to understand that you have a thoroughly developed idea, and that you are the best person to be taking on this challenge. They want some nuts and bolts, but do not want to be inundated with the daily operation of your business, unless this is a critical component of the nuts and bolts. Your financials, even a simple cash flow spreadsheet, will reveal the rest. Even when pitching a sale to a potential customer, several of these core topics are relevant.

Your presentation should be balanced by allocating equal amounts of time on each of the following:

Problem to be Solved
Your Solution
Your Team
Market Opportunity

Competition
Market Strategy
Current Status
Critical Risks
Financials
Funding Requirements

When combined into a presentation, these nine topics give an investor or donor a more complete view into your company or project. Let's take a brief look at each.

Problem to be Solved

You must prove that you have identified a problem that a well-defined target audience of paying customers would like to solve, or supporters would like to see solved. There are many neat ideas out there that have been shelved because they don't solve a critical problem, or the market for the idea is not well defined or understood.

Your Solution

Your product or service is the core of your business; therefore, you need to describe it in detail, right? Well, not exactly. At a first meeting, you should be able to describe your solution in one or two sentences, or on one or two slides if giving a formal presentation. In future meetings, you will have plenty of time to discuss the details of your widget.

Your Team

Who is involved with this widget? Who will run the company? Are you open to the investor/donor imposing advisors or managers, or even running the show? For most investors a solid team is the most important criteria before an investment is made. Don't sell your team short, but on the other hand, be up front about deficiencies that you might look to fill with help and expertise from your investor.

Market Opportunity

What is the size and growth potential of your market? Is the opportunity large enough to justify the size investment that you are seeking? In some cases, after carefully outlining this, it might make more sense to take out a loan, or self-finance some aspects of the business.

Competition

Who are your competitors? What is your competitive advantage and how will you ensure that your advantage is not replicated by the competition? Do you need patents? Is the timing of your widget launch critical? All of these items should be discussed in this section.

Market Strategy

Bringing your product or service to market requires a similar strategy to pitching your business. Today, with the growing popularity and effectiveness of web based sales channels and internet marketing, there are valuable market strategies that a current investor might not be familiar with. If this is important to your business, be able to defend these strategies as compared to more conventional sales channels.

Current Status

Investors and donors want to know whether your business is in the idea stage, or if you currently have products and services to sell, and customers who have already bought your widget. Be honest. If it will take six months before you have something to offer a customer, explain why. Do you need an infusion of funds to get through those six months, or do you need it at the launch?

Critical Risks

Identify what can go wrong and how you will manage the problems if they occur. Address actual versus perceived risks, and dispel those perceived risks with solid data. Not all investors/donors are experts in everything they invest in or donate to. Help them understand the current climate in your industry.

Financials

While full five-year financial projections are commonplace in comprehensive business plans, for new businesses they are taken with a grain of salt. Be realistic when working projections, and be as clear as possible as to where the funds will be used and why. Your financials should mirror all of the previous described items. In other words, someone should be able to pick up your financials, and understand the nature of how your business is run. Keep it simple, and boil it down to the fundamental income and expense categories that keep you running day to day. Draft up a simple spreadsheet outlining your business financials, and let the numbers do the talking. *Note: for practice and just plain good measure, track your personal financials in a similar manner including income from job(s) and living expenses. I can guarantee that you will expose many invaluable lessons for life!*

Funding Requirements

The final critical component to an investor or donor presentation is where you describe what or how much you are looking for. This may be all of the required funds, are part of them if you have another commitment. How much money do you need? Where are you going to use those funds? Will you need additional funds down the road? Most importantly, what do you have to offer in return?

If you can provide information to each of these topics in a convincing, confident, and honest manner, you will give potential investors or donors a clear view of your business, project, or widget.

My recommendation is to summarize all of this into a typed presentation of not more than 4-5 pages, AND a slide/Powerpoint presentation of not more than 15 slides. Have this available at all times, and pass it along to potential investors/donors as you open those first few doors.

Ask for feedback.

This information will help you refine your pitch, and your overall idea. Asking for feedback also lets your investor or donor know that you treat your relationships as partnerships and that you appreciate that mutual benefit is a critical piece of the puzzle.

Remember, despite you pouring your guts into this for countless sleepless nights, it is just a project – it doesn't define you. Wrap up that well-defined beginning, middle, and end into these few pages, and know when to run with it, take a break, or even put it down. The world has some funny ways about it, and when the time is right, you'll be ready.

In the meantime, grab a bowl of black beans.

Black Beans

Appendix 1 | Cooking Tips & Equivalents

General black bean cooking tips

1. Pick through dried beans to be sure there are no small twigs or stones.
2. Depending on the age of dried black beans, they could take 2 hours or longer to cook. Fresher dried beans will contain more moisture and cook in less time.
3. Pre-soaking black beans overnight will significantly reduce cooking time. Cover with 2 inches of water and allow for expansion in the container. Always drain and use fresh water before cooking.
4. In hot weather, refrigerate black beans while they soak to prevent fermentation.
5. Do not add salt or acidic ingredients such as lemon, vinegar, wine, and tomatoes until the beans are nearly done cooking. Adding earlier can cause the beans to get tough.
6. If additional water is needed during the cooking process, use hot water rather than cold water.

Cooking equivalents

1   cup dried black beans = 2 to 3 cups cooked black beans
1   pound dried beans = about 2 cups uncooked
1   pound dried beans = 5-1/2 to 6-1/2 cups cooked
1   16-ounce can black beans = 2 cups with liquid
1   16-ounce can black beans = 1-1/2 cups drained
2   cups cooked black beans = 6 servings

Black Beans

Appendix 2 | Health & Nutrition Information

All legumes are high in protein, and black beans are no exception. Dried beans are important sources of protein in vegetarian diets, and in areas where animal protein is scarce or expensive. However, not containing all nine amino acids, this protein is incomplete, so grains must also be a significant part of a vegetarian diet.

Black beans, as all dried beans, are also good sources of starches, fiber, B vitamins, iron, zinc, phosphorus, complex carbohydrates and calcium. Although, about half of the calcium in black beans is lost during cooking. High percentages of the other nutrients remain even after cooking.

Black Bean Nutrition Facts

Serving size	½ cup
Calories (from fat)	90 (5)
Total fat	0.5g (0%)
Saturated & Trans fat	0g
Cholesterol	0mg (0%)
Sodium	460mg (19%)
Total Carbs	19g (6%)
dietary fiber	6g (24%)
sugars	<1g
Protein	7g
Calcium	4%
Iron	10%

%'s are daily values based on a 2000 calorie diet.

Black Beans

Appendix 3 | Black Bean Resources

Much of the information about black beans found in Chapter 1 was collated from the following sources:

The Bean Bible
www.beanbible.com

About: Home Cooking
www.homecooking.about.com

US Dry Bean Council and the Bean Education & Awareness Network (B.E.A.N.)
www.americanbean.org

Goya
www.goya.com

Beans Around the World
www.beans-around-the-world.com

Food Reference Website
www.foodreference.com

Black Beans

About the Author

Michael is a freelance undersea specialist, entrepreneur, award-winning author, and explorer. His creation of 'Ocean Opportunity', a 501(c)3 not for profit organization, has afforded the vehicle to apply his innovative, grassroots model for business and exploration to many projects. Just one notable Success includes the 'Diving a Dream' project from 2004-2007 which was aired on NBC's Today Show in January 2007.

He is involved in numerous 'micro-ventures', and with each he has gone through the business development process, both for profit and not for profit, at various scales.

He currently serves as the Dive Safety Officer for the American Museum of Natural History in NYC, is a lifetime member of the American Academy of Underwater Sciences (AAUS), and routinely works in some of the most demanding environments on the planet.

His work in ocean advocacy went recognized as one of Rhode Island's '40 Under 40' by the Providence Business News in 2007. Later that year he earned membership in the prestigious Explorers Club. In 2010, Michael's work in deepwater exploration of the Bahamas was supported by the National Geographic Society.

Today, Michael is on a mission to take exploration and its influences on science, technology, and society where it has not yet ventured...to *oceana incognita*, while eating black beans to fuel his fire.

For more information, please visit:

Personal Website | Ocean Opportunity
http://www.oceanopportunity.com

Consulting Operations Website | Lombardi Undersea
http://www.lombardiundersea.com

Personal Blog | A New Life in the Sea
http://anewlifeinthesea.blogspot.com

To contact the author:

Michael Lombardi
PO Box 4668 #31885
New York, NY 10163
USA
explore@oceanopportunity.com